D1442990

Leaders
of World
War II

Stewart Ross

RAINTREE
STECK-VAUGHN
PUBLISHERS

A Harcourt Company

Austin   New York
www.steck-vaughn.com

THE WORLD WARS

Published by Raintree Steck-Vaughn Publishers,
an imprint of Steck-Vaughn Company

Library of Congress Cataloging-in-Publication Data
Ross, Stewart.
Leaders of World War II / Stewart Ross.
    p.   cm.—(The World Wars)
    Includes index.
    ISBN 0-7398-2756-1
    1. World War, 1939–1945—Biography—Juvenile literature.
    [1. World War, 1939–1945—Biography.]
    I. Title: Leaders of World War II. II. Title: Leaders of
World War II. III. Title. IV. Series.
    D736 .R66   2000
    940.53'092'2—dc21   00-059216

Printed in Italy. Bound in the United States.
1 2 3 4 5 6 7 8 9 0 05 04 03 02 01

Picture acknowledgments
AKG London 4, 5 (bottom), 6, 9,
21, 22, 24, 28, 31, 32, 36, 38, 47,
49, 51, 53, 58, 59; Hodder
Wayland Picture Library/© IWM 5
(top); 7, 8, 11, 20, 23 (bottom),
25, 34, 39, 42, 43; Peter Newark's
Military Pictures 13, 18, 23 (top),
29, 30, 35, 41, 44, 45, 46, 48, 52,
54, 55, 57; Popperfoto 10, 12, 14,
15, 16 (top & bottom), 19, 26, 27,
33, 37, 40, 50, 56
Cover photographs:
Churchill by Yousuf Karsh (Camera
Press); Hitler (Hodder Wayland
Picture Library); Roosevelt (AKG,
London); Stalin (AKG, London)

Contents

Leaders and Leadership

Churchill, Hitler, Stalin, Roosevelt, de Gaulle ... World War II featured some of the most colorful leaders in modern history. They were all ambitious and forceful men. A few were honorable. Many were unscrupulous, and a number were ruthlessly cruel. Together they had a huge impact on the course of the war and thus on the shape of the modern world. All major war leaders shared certain qualities. They did not normally shirk from making tough decisions. They were also known as planners and powerful communicators. Above all, they all had that indefinable something in their character that demanded respect and obedience and made them symbols of their cause.

Poster power: clever propaganda made Hitler appear younger and larger than he really was.

There were three categories of war leaders: politician, military commander, and figurehead. The most influential (Churchill, Roosevelt, Hitler, Stalin, and Mussolini) combined aspects of all three roles. The requirements of total war gave these men, both democrats and autocrats, massive authority.

Elected leaders wielded less direct power than the dictators. The U.S. Constitution, for instance, did not allow Roosevelt to declare war. However, because some democratic rights were shelved during wartime (Great Britain postponed its parliamentary elections for five years), even democratic leaders had greater powers than did their peacetime counterparts. The power of the dictators was limited by the need for advice and assistance. Even the megalomaniac Stalin was forced to rely heavily (if reluctantly) on the military skill of Marshal Zhukov.

Two figureheads

Japan's Emperor Hirohito and Great Britain's King George VI were constitutional leaders who left the practical conduct of the war to others. George VI supported Prime Minister Winston Churchill and made morale-boosting public appearances. Hirohito, to whom Japanese officers pledged absolute obedience, played a similarly symbolic role until August 1945, when he broke with tradition and broadcast the order that his people should surrender.

In contrast to the totalitarian leaders, Churchill liked to give an impression of relaxed determination.

Franklin D. Roosevelt, the leader of the Allied coalition, played a card game called Patience to help him relax at times of great tension.

Corporal in Command

Concentrating political and military power in a single leader gave unity of purpose and quick decision-making. But it had serious drawbacks. Hitler, a World War I corporal, showed this when the German invasion of the USSR ran into difficulties in 1941. His interference (notably when he diverted troops away from the drive toward Moscow in July 1941, thereby probably saving the Soviet capital) infuriated his field commanders and reduced his army's effectiveness.

What made the World War II leaders so memorable? Many were passionate men devoted to their democratic, fascist, or communist ideologies. Second, as the war was often one of rapid movement over vast areas, it promoted leaders of imagination and flair. This was in sharp contrast to the dogged commanders of World War I. Finally, to a greater extent than World War I, this war was fought with the media (press, radio, and film) as well as with the gun. This played into the hands of image-conscious leaders, like Hitler.

5

Winston Churchill (1874–1965)

Churchill as a young army officer, 1895. When he became prime minister in 1940, he was widely experienced in military, as well as political, affairs.

By 1939, the sixty-five-year-old Winston Churchill had enjoyed a long and controversial career as a popular Liberal journalist, soldier, and senior Conservative politician. He had not had a job in government for ten years, and many believed he would never have one again. Remarkably, his finest hour was yet to come.

As the symbol of his nation's resistance in the early years of the war, Churchill made a point of meeting as many service men and women as possible.

Misjudgment and misfortunes played into Churchill's hands. During the 1930s, he warned that Prime Minister Neville Chamberlain's policy of appeasement toward Nazi Germany would merely postpone the inevitable conflict. In 1939, when his gloomy prediction came true, support for Churchill was growing fast. During the "phony war," he used his position as First Lord of the Admiralty to urge in vain that Great Britain and France prepare more vigilantly for the onslaught ahead. Immediately after German forces smashed into the Low Countries on May 10, 1940, Chamberlain resigned. When Lord Halifax refused the post, Churchill became prime minister and leader of his country. His skills, experience, and interests made him the ideal leader at such a difficult moment.

Churchill was enormously single-minded and determined. His principal aim, from which he never wavered, was to defeat Nazi Germany. To this end, he was prepared to employ almost any tactic or strategy. He sanctioned "saturation bombing" (see panel), and ordered an attack on the French fleet to keep it from falling into German hands.

Sir Arthur Harris (1892–1984)

Air Chief Marshal "Bomber" Harris, commander-in-chief of the RAF's Bomber Command, was perhaps Great Britain's most controversial war leader. In 1941, he was ordered to begin "area bombing" to smash German industry and break civilian morale. He then developed "saturation bombing" (sending hundreds of bombers on a gigantic raid on a single city). The strategy had limited success. German industrial output rose during 1942–44, and, after the war, Harris was held responsible by some for the deaths of hundreds of thousands of civilians.

Realizing that Great Britain alone could not defeat the Nazis, Churchill sought every available ally. He deliberately and unashamedly courted President Roosevelt and the American people. To get and keep the United States on his side, he flattered, cajoled, and joked with them. A plan was put forward to hand over British bases in the Caribbean to the U.S. Navy. In exchange, Great Britain would be given several much-needed warships. Churchill was reluctant to do this at first, but, by September 1940, the deal was done. Nine U.S. destroyers were handed over to the British.

Churchill was no admirer of communism. Even so, during the 1930s, he had called in vain for an anti-German pact with Stalin, the leader of the communist USSR. When Hitler launched his surprise attack on the Soviet Union in 1941, Churchill immediately offered the besieged Soviets British support. This was the beginning of his "Grand Alliance" of Great Britain, the United States, and the USSR.

As well as single-mindedness, Churchill possessed considerable political skills. To get broad party support, he formed a coalition government from all but the extreme wings of the Conservative, Labour, and Liberal parties. His five-man war cabinet, including himself as prime minister and minister of defense, contained both Labour and Conservative leaders. To woo the working classes, he appointed trade-union leader Ernest Bevin as minister of labor.

Despite the heavy bombing of Great Britain's cities in 1940–41 (pictured here the devastated Coventry Cathedral), Churchill managed to inspire the British people to believe they could win the war.

Churchill, a skilled parliamentarian, worked hard to keep the House of Commons on his side. It was not always easy. In July 1942, for example, he faced serious opposition over massive losses suffered by a convoy to the Soviet Union. He showed respect for his cabinet and military leaders. He used every tactic to get his own way (usually successfully) but never overrode the collective judgment of his senior advisers or colleagues.

Although his health deteriorated markedly toward the end of the war, Churchill was blessed with enormous energy. Aided by afternoon naps, he often worked around the clock. No detail was too slight for his attention. His continuous questioning and interference frequently irritated those who worked with him, but it did keep everyone on their toes.

When fit, Churchill was an energetic traveler, inspecting bomb sites, coastal defenses, and fighter stations. He flew over 23,400 mi. (36,000 km) to visit troops in the field and hold talks with Allied leaders. Most significant were his meeting with Roosevelt in Newfoundland (1941) and the "Big Three" conferences with Roosevelt and Stalin (Tehran, 1943, and Yalta, 1945).

Churchill's famous "never surrender" speech to the House of Commons on June 4, 1940, cleverly combined a rallying cry to the British with a plea for American help:

"We shall fight on the beaches, we shall fight on the landing grounds, we shall fight in the fields and in the streets, we shall fight in the hills; we shall never surrender; and even if ... this Island ... were subjugated and starving, then our Empire beyond the seas ... would carry on the struggle, until, in God's good time, the New World, with all its power and might, steps forth to the rescue and the liberation of the Old."

Winston S. Churchill,
The Second World War, vol. II.

The "Big Three" (left to right) Churchill, Roosevelt, and Stalin at Yalta in 1945

Churchill was an instinctive master of propaganda with a remarkable ability to reflect and shape the national mood. At key moments, from the time he took office ("I have nothing to offer but blood, toil, tears, and sweat") to the victory at El Alamein ("This is not the end. It is not even the beginning of the end. But it is, perhaps, the end of the beginning") he invariably came up with an appropriate and moving phrase. He was at his most powerful in the grim days of 1940, when his words of brave defiance, delivered in a gruff, slow voice, lifted the spirits of an entire nation. Churchill matched his words with a bulldog-like public image. The hunched, determined stance, the cigar, and the V-sign for victory were always the same, memorable and reassuring. It was pure showmanship, but it worked.

Churchill was at his best during the first two critical years of his premiership. Thereafter, his physical condition deteriorated, and he was increasingly overshadowed by Stalin and Roosevelt. Indeed, there was always a degree of rivalry between Churchill and Roosevelt that Stalin skillfully exploited. Significantly, during the 1943 Tehran Conference, Roosevelt had private talks with Stalin but not with Churchill.

Unprepared for the challenges of peace, Churchill's Conservative party was defeated in the general election of July 1945. For a few

Churchill's steady gaze and jutting jaw seemed to reflect the true spirit of the "British bulldog."

The personal touch

The close friendship between Prime Minister Churchill and President Roosevelt impacted significantly on Allied strategy. In 1942–43, for example, Stalin and the U.S. chiefs-of-staff were calling for a swift Allied invasion of Northern Europe. Churchill, who believed it was too early to open this "Second Front," exploited his relationship with Roosevelt to get the cross-Channel invasion postponed until 1944.

"Want a light, guv?" Churchill's large cigar—lighted or not—was a carefully chosen part of his image.

One of Churchill's most endearing traits was his ironic British sense of humor. Thus he recorded his reaction to news of his 1945 election defeat:

By noon [on 26 July] it was clear that the Socialists would have a majority. At luncheon my wife said to me, "It may well be a blessing in disguise." I replied, "At the moment it seems quite effectively disguised."

Winston S. Churchill, *The Second World War,* vol. VI.

years, he busied himself with writing and seeking to influence the priorities of the postwar world. His second premiership (1951–55) was undistinguished, although he showed occasional flashes of his old fire. When he died in January 1965, he was given a state funeral. Almost the entire world paid tribute to one of the most flamboyant, charismatic, and, arguably, the most admired of all the Allied war leaders.

Dwight D. Eisenhower (1890–1969)

The Allied victory in 1945 was a triumph of diplomacy as well as arms. As senior military figures needed to operate within a multinational alliance, they were inevitably drawn into politics. A few displayed the necessary diplomacy, but one was outstanding. He was U.S. General Dwight Eisenhower, chosen in 1944 as the Supreme Commander of the Allied Expeditionary Force in Europe.

"Ike," as Eisenhower was popularly known, had one very unusual quality for a war leader: almost everyone liked him. His popularity was not engineered by rallies or fostered by dramatic radio speeches. It stemmed directly from his courteous, open, and honest manner. In the words of the professional diplomat George Kennan, he was "the nation's number one Boy Scout."

Eisenhower's remarkable ability to get along with everyone he met was one of his greatest assets.

In 1933, Eisenhower's personal and organizational talents were recognized by chief of the army staff, General Douglas MacArthur, who made him his aide. When the United States entered the war in 1941, Eisenhower was singled out by General George C. Marshall to head the War Plans Division in Washington, D.C. His enthusiasm for an early Allied cross-Channel invasion (code-named Roundup) brought him into contact with President Roosevelt and Prime Minister Churchill.

U.S. armor rolls ashore during Operation Torch, the Allied landings in North Africa, 1942. This was Eisenhower's first major command.

By the age of fifty-two, Eisenhower had charmed a string of powerful men (MacArthur, Marshall, Roosevelt, and Churchill) and had shown himself an able theoretical strategist in war games and his Roundup plans. Now it was time for Eisenhower to prove himself in the field. In June 1942, he was appointed over the heads of 366 senior officers to command U.S. troops in Europe. Five months later, he was given the overall command of Operation Torch, the Allied invasion of French North Africa.

Eisenhower's handling of this tricky operation makes an excellent case study of his qualities as a war leader. He

In contrast to many other more bombastic war leaders, Eisenhower was always prepared to admit that his achievements were based on the efforts of others. He expressed this most memorably in a speech made in London in June 1945:

Humility must always be the portion of any man who receives acclaim earned in the blood of his followers and sacrifices of his friends.

The Times, June 13, 1945.

showed first-class organizational skills in getting two huge convoys, one from the United States and a second from the UK, to land troops in three places at the same time. The eventual Allied success in May 1943, although executed by his deputy, General Harold Alexander, also owed much to Eisenhower's overall leadership.

To neutralize Anglo-American rivalries, Eisenhower filled each position in his HQ with two men, one British and one American. An even greater problem was the attitude of Vichy France, the regime that had come to terms with the Nazis to avoid occupation. Eisenhower had no way of knowing how the 100,000 Vichy troops stationed in Morocco, Algeria, and Tunisia would react to his invading forces.

The key to the situation was Admiral Jean Darlan, the French commander in North Africa. After approaching Eisenhower and Hitler, Darlan eventually decided to support the Americans. Eisenhower immediately overlooked Darlan's past and recognized his authority in the region. Although de Gaulle and others condemned this, Eisenhower's prompt action neutralized the bulk of the Vichy forces and saved many Allied lives. Roosevelt and Churchill both believed the "temporary expedient" had been the right thing to do.

George C. Marshall (1880–1959)

Aloof, intelligent, and a brilliant administrator, Marshall was heralded by Winston Churchill as "the organizer of victory." He was appointed U.S. Army Chief of Staff on September 1, 1939, and promptly set about turning the country's force of 200,000 men into one capable of fighting, and winning, a world war. In under four years he had created a well-equipped, well-trained, and well-led army of more than 8 million soldiers serving throughout the world.

Eisenhower with the Allied Supreme Command that planned Operation Overlord, the Allied landings in northern Europe in 1943

The success of Operation Torch made Eisenhower the obvious choice for overall command of the invasion of Sicily in July 1943 and the move into Italy in September. These operations again fully tested Eisenhower's powers. London wanted Allied efforts concentrated on the Mediterranean while Washington (urged on by Stalin) hankered after a cross-Channel invasion, so Eisenhower's Mediterranean campaigns had no overall strategic objective. Equally trying was the rivalry between the cautious British General Bernard Montgomery and the flamboyant American General George Patton, whose loyal forces sometimes seemed to dislike each other as much as the enemy.

In spring 1943, the Allies started to prepare for the invasion of France (Operation Overlord). Eisenhower was appointed Supreme Commander of the Overlord forces. The subsequent D-Day landings and drive into Germany were Eisenhower's outstanding achievements as a war leader.

Uneasy allies—Eisenhower (next to the tank) and Montgomery (nearest the camera) watch gunnery training shortly before D-Day, 1944.

Berlin, here we come! U.S. reinforcements moving inland shortly after the D-Day landings

It would be foolish to give all the credit for Allied success in Northwest Europe to a single man. It was the work of thousands of commanders, soldiers, airmen, sailors, planners, organizers, and administrators. Nevertheless, it was Eisenhower who bore the final responsibility for the operation's success or failure.

It was he who made the brave decision to launch the invasion on June 6, 1944, even though the poor weather conditions reduced its chances of success. It was he, too, who had to mediate among his generals, Omar Bradley, Patton, and Montgomery. He also had the almost impossible task of balancing French, British, and American interests.

As if this was not enough, from September onward Eisenhower was in direct command of operations in the field. In this role he gambled successfully

Eisenhower (left) with General Patton, his highly talented field commander

by pushing rapidly east rather than consolidating along the River Seine, as originally planned. His most testing moment came in the winter of 1944–45, when the Germans made a surprise counterattack in strength through the Ardennes (the Battle of the Bulge). When he realized what was happening, Eisenhower reacted with cool efficiency, swiftly moving up reinforcements to retake the initiative.

By the time Germany surrendered on May 7, Eisenhower was a hero throughout the free world. His career was by no means over, however. He supervised the withdrawal of U.S. troops, wrote his memoirs, and served as President of Columbia University and Supreme Commander of NATO. Finally, in 1952, he was elected President of the United States. In many ways, his wartime experience (decision-making, planning, conciliating, and organizing) had been ideal training for his presidency and, not surprisingly, he was reelected for a second term in 1956.

Failure of diplomacy

Eisenhower's abilities were not always perfect. In January 1945, the Germans counterattacked through Alsace. Without informing the French forces, who were under the overall command of de Gaulle, Eisenhower drew up plans for the abandonment of Strasbourg, a symbol of Franco-German rivalry. When de Gaulle found out, there was such an intense fight between the French and the Americans that Churchill had to fly to France to sort it out. In the end, Strasbourg was not abandoned.

Charles de Gaulle (1890–1970)

Charles de Gaulle, a fiercely patriotic, intellectual brigadier-general in the French army, fled to England in 1940. From there, he appealed to the French people to continue the war under his leadership. Condemned as a traitor in France and frequently at odds with the British government, he formed the Free French Forces in exile and worked closely with resistance movements within France. In August 1944 he entered a now-liberated Paris and set up a provisional government. From this time on, his political skill and prestige as a wartime leader enabled him to dominate postwar France.

Adolf Hitler (1889–1945)

More words have been spoken and written about Hitler than any other war leader. Even today, more than half a century since his death, he continues to fascinate and appall. But just how talented a leader was he, and what was the secret of his influence?

Right: Hitler the actor is superbly captured in this early, menacing photograph.

To judge by his early career, Hitler's talents were very limited indeed. He failed at school and as an artist. Only when he became involved in politics in the 1920s did he find his true vocation. Enthusiastic, alarmingly single-minded, and a brilliant speaker, he rose to lead the Nazi party and then, in 1933, his country. In power he ruthlessly crushed all opposition, surrounded himself with loyal followers, and restored his country's belief in itself through nationalism and the promise of more jobs and a better standard of living.

There has never been any doubt about Hitler's great strength as a leader—his ability to inspire others to follow him. Even generals who scorned his strategic ineptitude, like Rommel, admitted that his men were prepared to "sacrifice themselves to the last man" for their beloved führer, or leader. But, in the end, leadership is about more than inspiration. It involves wise decision–making, flexibility, careful planning, and clever appointments. In these areas, Hitler was found to be increasingly wanting.

The making of a dictator— Hitler, in characteristically aggressive pose, addressing a Nazi rally in 1933

Not many war leaders, possibly not even Churchill, could match Hitler as a public speaker. As Otto Strasser, who saw him in action, wrote:

Hitler responds to the vibrations of the human heart with the delicacy of a seismograph ... enabling him, with a certainty with which no conscious gift could endow him, to act as a loudspeaker proclaiming the most secret desires, ... the sufferings and personal revolts of a whole nation ... speaking as the spirit moves him ... he is ... transformed into one of the greatest speakers of the century.

Otto Strasser, *Hitler and I*, London, 1940

Hitler's downfall began in September 1939, with the outbreak of the European war that he had hoped would not happen. Despite early successes, the conflict exposed Hitler's weaknesses as a leader and brought his planned "One Thousand Year Reich" to its end.

Until 1942, it looked as if Hitler's leadership was as potent in war as it had been in peace. Drawing on the new-found confidence the führer had inspired, Germany swept aside all enemies, except Great Britain , and drove deep into the Soviet Union. The triumphant campaigns of 1940 owed much to Hitler's strong support for a dynamic "lightning war" (blitzkrieg). And his stubborn determination, displayed in refusal to consider withdrawal during the winter of 1941–42, probably saved his forces in Russia.

Hitler's aggression could be used against him, as in this Allied propaganda poster of 1941.

"Evil genius"

The highly competent German general Franz Halder recalled the one, overriding force in Hitler's life:

Even at the height of his power there was for him no Germany, there were no German troops for whom he felt himself responsible; for him there was (at first subconsciously, but in his last years fully consciously) only one greatness, a greatness which dominated his life and to which his evil genius sacrificed everything (his own Ego).

Cited in Alan Bullock, *Hitler: A Study in Tyranny*, London, 1952

These spectacular early achievements held the seeds of future disaster, for they led Hitler to believe in his own invincibility and the sureness of his judgment. This produced many unwise, even foolish, decisions from the "Bohemian corporal," as some of his generals secretly called Hitler, who took overall command of the army in December 1941.

Even in 1940, when Hitler held back his tanks and allowed the British to organize their evacuation from Dunkirk, there were signs that his interference in military matters might not always be beneficial. Examples multiplied in the years that followed.

Believing the Soviet Union would collapse before the winter, he refused to allow his soldiers to take cold weather clothing with them on Operation Barbarossa (1941). In 1942, obsessed with his Russian campaign, he missed an opportunity for decisive victory in North Africa. The following year his refusal to withdraw contributed to the disaster at Stalingrad. And, as the war ground toward its terrible end, his paranoid refusal to accept the inevitable led to the wholesale destruction of his country.

"One People, One State, One Leader!"
Hitler at a Nuremberg rally, 1937

Field Marshal Karl Rudolf Gerd von Rundstedt (1875–1953)

After retiring in 1938, Rundstedt's remarkable wartime career began when Hitler reinstated him to plan the invasion of Poland and lead the invasion of France. He was dismissed in November 1941 for ordering his soldiers to withdraw on the Russian front. Restored four months later, by 1944 he was commanding German forces resisting the Allied invasion of Normandy. His wartime service didn't end there—the indispensable field marshal was called upon to supervise the German retreat and then to lead the counterattack in the Ardennes. He finally retired for good in 1945.

Hitler frequently allowed his personal prejudices to get in the way of sensible strategic thinking. The invasion of Yugoslavia shortly before the launch of Operation Barbarossa was, at best, unwise. Equally foolish was the harsh treatment of the Ukrainians, who at first regarded the German invaders as liberators.

Inmates march to work in the Dachau concentration camp. Hitler's racism poisoned Germany and every country the Nazis occupied.

Furthermore, Hitler failed to channel his resources effectively into the war effort. The forced labor of subject peoples, for example, was inefficient as well as a gross breach of their human rights. Equally dubious in economic terms was the private business arm (WVHA) of Himmler's SS, which made huge profits from enterprises ranging from jam-making to armaments production.

Add to these faults Hitler's unpredictable and sometimes ill-advised appointments and his erratic behavior under pressure, and one might wonder why he lasted so long as a war leader. But that overlooks three things.

The July Bomb Plot

There had always been opposition to Hitler within Germany. In 1944, when the Axis powers were clearly losing the war, a group of conspirators led by Count von Stauffenberg tried to blow up the führer in his East Prussian headquarters, the Wolf's Lair. On July 20, a time bomb left in a briefcase caused considerable damage but left Hitler relatively unscathed. Hundreds of suspects were rounded up, tortured, and executed. It is said that Hitler had some of the more grisly executions filmed for private viewing.

In step with the führer: Himmler and Hitler in 1938

Heinrich Himmler (1900–1945)

An ex-soldier and poultry farmer, Himmler's war record was one of unmitigated horror and disaster. He used his command of the SS and the Gestapo to exterminate the Jews and other "unwanted" minorities, resulting in over 6 million deaths of Jews alone. His downfall began in 1944, when Hitler made him commander-in-chief of the home forces. An incompetent military commander, he could do nothing to halt the Russian advance and was dismissed two days before Hitler's suicide. His attempt to escape in disguise was foiled by the British military police, and he took poison before he could be brought to trial.

First, the economic recovery and military triumphs of 1933–1941 had filled a deep well of goodwill toward Hitler that was slow to seep away. Second, for some time Hitler's weaknesses were masked by the strength, talents, and determination of the nation he led and by the many able men who served under him. Finally, only at the very end did the führer lose the hypnotic personal magnetism that had brought him to office and given him such power over almost everyone with whom he came into contact.

Hitler congratulates a twelve-year-old after awarding him the Iron Cross for bravery, April 1945. Many young German boys, raised in the Hitler Youth, fought to defend their fatherland as the Allies closed in.

Field Marshal Bernard Montgomery (1887–1976)

Clearly talented but immodest and painfully undiplomatic, Montgomery (or "Monty," as he was popularly known) was one of Great Britain's most controversial army commanders. His flamboyant personality and outspoken manner ran contrary to his battle tactics, which were generally cautious.

Montgomery became a popular hero in Great Britain after his success at El Alamein in 1942. It is worth mentioning, however, that the victory rested on foundations laid by General Claude Auchinleck and Field Marshal Harold Alexander and was achieved with massive superiority in men and material. Montgomery's chief contribution to the victory was perhaps not his handling of the battle but the way he had rallied his troops after months of morale-sapping retreat, instilling them with a belief that Rommel could be beaten.

Monty in North Africa, November 1942

British 25-pounder guns in action at the battle of El Alamein, 1942. Montgomery made sure he had a massive superiority in armaments before the battle began.

Caution was the hallmark of Montgomery's next major campaign—the invasion of Sicily in July 1943. At Montgomery's insistence, Eisenhower changed the plan for an American landing near Palermo in the northwest to a massed landing on the other side of the island. This cut the risk of failure but left the Allies to fight their way across Sicily, resulting in heavy casualties. Montgomery's role in the invasion of Italy was similarly conservative.

El Alamein

El Alamein was the site of three battles fought between July and November 1942. In the first, General Auchinleck halted Rommel's eastward advance. The second, fought by Alexander and Montgomery, beat off a German attack. The result of the third and most famous battle was almost a foregone conclusion. With 230,000 men and 1,200 tanks facing Rommel's 80,000 men (many of whom, including the commander himself, were sick) and 540 tanks, Alexander and Montgomery secured the Allies' first major land victory of the war.

25

Montgomery was at his most controversial during the famous 1944–45 campaigns in Northwest Europe. With overall command of British land forces, he was frequently at odds with the Americans, particularly Patton (his arch rival), Bradley, and Eisenhower. While they favored a coordinated advance along a wide front, he wanted Allied strength concentrated on a single, narrow front

(commanded by himself). That said, during the Battle of the Bulge, Eisenhower had sufficient confidence in Montgomery's abilities to place all Allied forces to the north of the German advance (including two U.S. armies) under the Englishman's command.

Allies but not friends: Montgomery and his supreme commander, General Eisenhower, in 1944.

Montgomery's reputation has suffered since his death. His self-confidence now appears arrogant and his rivalry with Patton as unnecessary and unworthy. His methodical tactics, favoring frontal assault above maneuver, are uncomfortably reminiscent of World War I commanders. Beside the brilliant Rommel and the dashing Patton, he appears dull, almost second-rate.

He made errors of judgment too. The failure of the northward drive from Antwerp in the autumn of 1944 was ultimately his responsibility. Earlier, he had made a major tactical mistake when trying to capture the town of Caen in July. His massive tank attack on a narrow front across the Orne River was a costly failure. Nor did he help himself afterward by claiming that his real aim had been to secure his position and

Field Marshal Harold Alexander (1891–1969)

Alexander was an able soldier-diplomat in the Eisenhower mold. He skillfully negotiated the withdrawals at Dunkirk and from Burma, provided the material for the victory at El Alamein (1942), and, as operational commander, oversaw the conquest of North Africa and the landings in Sicily and Italy. After Churchill had rejected Eisenhower's request for his transfer to Northwest Europe, Great Britain's most respected army commander remained bogged down in the under-resourced Italian campaign.

divert German attention so the Americans could advance to his right. It is now clear that although this is indeed what happened, it was not what he had originally planned.

Valid though these criticisms may be, they ignore two important points. First, by mid-1942 the British public had endured three years of almost uninterrupted gloom. Their ships had been sunk, their cities blitzed, their colonies lost, and their armies defeated almost everywhere. They were desperate for a victory and a hero. Montgomery gave them both. Did it really matter that he achieved it through careful planning and cautious tactics?

Second, although Montgomery was not an inspired battle tactician, neither did he try to act like one. He did what had to be done, sensibly, within his limitations. If the main task of a commander is to defeat his enemy, then he performed that task with regularity. Whatever his personal failings, it was no mean achievement.

Strategy or politics?

After the Allied advance from Normandy in August 1944, Montgomery, commanding the British forces in the north, said that with massive backing he could end the war that year. Patton made similar claims for his forces (under the overall command of General Bradley) farther south. Eisenhower was eager that progress toward Germany should not become an Anglo-American race and opted for advance along a broad front. This may not have been the best strategy, but at least it curbed the potentially dangerous Montgomery-Patton rivalry.

A leader's triumph—Montgomery reading surrender terms to the German commanders facing the British front, 1945

27

Benito Mussolini (1883–1945)

There was an air of tragi-comedy about Mussolini as a wartime leader. In peacetime he talked much of war, praising its virtues and promising glory for Italy when the conflict came. His prophecies were partially, if superficially, fulfilled by Italy's successful conquest of Abyssinia (Ethiopia) in 1936. But when the major conflict broke out in 1939, he was reluctant to join in. And when he eventually did, it brought ruin for his country and humiliation and death for himself. What went wrong?

When Mussolini wrote so glowingly of the virtues of war in 1932, he little realized that, in ten years' time, war would be his own undoing:

Fascism ... believes neither in the possibility nor the utility of perpetual peace. It thus repudiates the doctrine of Pacifism ... War alone brings up to its highest tension all human energy and puts the stamp of nobility upon the peoples who have the courage to meet it.

From the entry on "Fascism" in an Italian Encyclopedia, 1932

Mussolini addresses the Italian people, 1929. The casual attitude of his followers contrasts sharply with Hitler's supporters in similar situations.

Mussolini was a brilliant propagandist. It was his greatest talent as a leader. But, in the end, he became the victim of his own propaganda. His grand claims were nothing but a great deal of exaggeration, deception, and falsehood. In war, as he feared before he committed himself to it, there is nowhere to hide. It found him out.

Examples of Mussolini's propaganda are not hard to find. He came to power in 1922 after a train journey to Rome followed by a grand parade of fascists. His mythology soon combined the two into a "March on Rome." Mussolini himself was not simply prime minister; he was "Il Duce"—the leader. He turned an effort to preserve the value of Italian currency into a "Battle for the Lire" and a push to increase the size of the country's population into a "Battle for Births." Everything he did was made to sound grand and splendid. In a country where opposition was forbidden, the truth was easily hidden.

Follow your leader—an Italian painting of Mussolini's bodyguards, all of whom look like Il Duce

29

W HITLER   W MVSSOLINI

PACE CIVILTA LAVORO

ANNO   XVI

An Italian postcard commemorating the German–Italian fascist alliance of 1938

Mussolini was a bully. To gain easy popularity before 1940, he picked on external victims he knew he could crush—the Greeks in Corfu, the Yugoslavs in Fiume, the Abyssinians, and the Albanians. The forces he built up were sufficient for these sideshows. But, like their "Duce," they were strong on show and weak on substance. Italy's ships were fast but poorly armored; her fascist army commanders were politically correct but of dubious ability; her air force, the pride of Europe in the early 1930s, had declined markedly by 1940. For all of this, the country's dictator was ultimately responsible. Not surprisingly, therefore, Mussolini hesitated to join Germany in war against Great Britain , France, and the other Allies. His military and economic advisers said Italy was not ready for a major conflict. His people did not want it, and, in private, "Il Duce" was scornful of their stomach for battle. So why, in June 1940, did he commit Italy to the European war?

A rare victory

Mussolini recognized that the Italian colonies in East Africa—Eritrea, Italian Somaliland, and Abyssinia—were a convenient springboard for attacks on British and French territories in the region. In August 1940, a huge Italian force commanded by the Duke of Aosta, a cousin of the king, swiftly overran British and French Somaliland. But Mussolini did not enjoy the fruits of his rare victory for long—by May the following year British, South African, and East African forces had crushed Aosta and captured all of Italy's East African empire.

The fascist brotherhood

Although Hitler and Mussolini did not get on when they first met in 1934, the relationship between the two men later improved, leading to the Axis Treaty (1936) and Pact of Steel (1939). Hitler showed an unusual loyalty toward his fellow fascist leader, supporting him even in defeat. Following his removal by the Fascist Grand Council in 1943, Mussolini was put under house arrest in a hotel high in the Apennine Mountains. From here, German airborne troops rescued him in a daring raid, involving crash-landing their gliders on the mountainside and flew him to Munich. It was at Hitler's suggestion that Mussolini became head of a second, short-lived, fascist republic in the north of Italy.

Mussolini was ashamed of his inactivity, jealous of Hitler's triumphs, and, now that the fighting seemed nearly over, he believed he could collect a few rich pickings from the Nazi feast. It was a terrible mistake. Apart from a few early successes against tiny forces in East Africa, Mussolini's war was a tale of almost continual disaster.

The Italian navy, ill coordinated with the air force and lacking aircraft carriers, was no match for the Royal Navy in the Mediterranean. The gains in East Africa were swiftly reversed. The badly led offensives in Greece and North Africa both had to be swiftly rescued by the Germans. Defeated and bankrupt, within a year Italy had become little more than a dependency of the Third Reich.

Hitler (nearest the camera) and Mussolini meet in East Prussia, 1941. By now Hitler was beginning to see the Italian alliance more as a hindrance than a help.

King Victor Emmanuel III (1869–1947)

Victor Emmanuel was an uninspiring figurehead monarch who believed it his duty to abide by the wishes of career politicians. Nevertheless, at two points in his life, he had an important influence on politics. The first was in 1922, when he refused to sign a decree introducing martial law. Had he done so, Mussolini and his Fascist Party would probably never have come to power. The second came twenty-two years later, when he ordered the disgraced Mussolini to be arrested. Despite this, he was tainted by his association with fascism, and, in 1946, following his abdication, the Italian people voted for an end to the monarchy.

Mussolini's leadership had been responsible for getting Italy into this predicament and it was also responsible for making it worse. His decision to send troops to fight beside the Germans in the Soviet Union and to declare war on the United States made little sense. Nor did many of the commands he sent to his generals in the field—all too often they were based upon what he wished were happening rather than reality.

When King Victor Emmanuel III wrote to Mussolini in July 1943 explaining why the Fascist Grand Council had decided to dismiss their long-standing leader, his tone was polite but chillingly blunt:

My dear Mussolini, it is no longer any good. Italy has gone to pieces. The soldiers don't want to fight any more ... you are the most hated man in Italy!

Cited in C. K. Macdonald, *The Second World War*

King Victor Emmanuel III, who listened to the wishes of his people and ordered Mussolini's arrest in 1943

By 1942, King Victor Emmanuel III and those close to him were looking for a way to take Italy out of the unpopular war. The next year, following the successful Allied invasion of Sicily, the Fascist Grand Council dismissed Mussolini. To many people's surprise, the king then had him arrested. Rescued by the Germans, Mussolini returned for a short time to govern a makeshift fascist state in northern Italy. Finally, in April 1945, as he was attempting to flee to Germany, he was captured by his own people and shot.

In the early years, there had been some substance to Mussolini's leadership. He had, at least, restored order to his country and given it a sense of well-being. But much of what he did had been gesture, and, when war came, that was nowhere near enough.

The price of failure—Mussolini (center), his mistress, and a supporter were strung up after their execution by Italian partisans.

Field Marshal Erwin Rommel (1891–1944)

Speaking to the House of Commons about the North African campaign in January 1942, Churchill declared, "We have a very daring and skilful opponent against us, and, may I say across the havoc of war, a great general." The prime minister was heavily criticized for openly praising an enemy leader, but no one denied the truth of his words. Everyone, both the Allies and their enemies, recognized that Rommel was indeed a "great general."

Rommel, unlike many of his contemporary officers, did not come from the traditional Prussian officer class. His promotion depended on his exceptional abilities rather than breeding. He demonstrated his high intelligence in a book on tactics, *Infantry Attacks*, and in the successful way he adapted to mechanized warfare when put in charge of the 7th Panzer Division in 1940. In the desert war, by closely studying his opponents' tactics, he was often able to second guess their moves and so surprise them with his own.

Rommel, the highly respected German field commander of the war

The Ghost Division

Shortly before the attack on France, Hitler put Rommel in command of the 7th Panzer Division. The Army High Command objected strongly because Rommel had no experience with armored forces. But the führer stuck by his man, and Rommel soon proved the wisdom of his decision. Adapting to the new high-speed warfare, he swept through France with a series of maneuvers that brought him over 50,000 prisoners. The French, astounded by the ability of the 7th Panzer Division to turn up where least expected and then disappear again at high speed, nicknamed them the "Ghost Division."

Rommel was blessed with boundless energy, a quality common to many war leaders. A German paratroop officer, himself a ski champion before the war, recalled Rommel with admiration:

He had the strength of a horse.
I never saw another man like him.
No need for food, no need for drink,
no need for sleep. He could wear out
men twenty and thirty years younger.
If anything, he was too hard,
on himself and everyone else.

Cited in Desmond Young,
Rommel: The Desert Fox

Rommel as a young soldier. He was awarded the Iron Cross for gallantry during World War I.

There was much more to Rommel than just brains. He was energetic, daring, and brave. He was wounded several times in World War I and once led six infantry companies 2,100 ft. (650 m) up a mountain to capture 9,000 Italian troops and 81 guns. During his World War II campaigns in North Africa, although now a senior general, he made a point of appearing in the front line to encourage his men and share their dangers.

In May 1940, Rommel took his Panzers from the Belgian border to Cambrai in a week, right through the French lines, ignoring the threat to his flanks and supply lines. When transferred to North Africa in 1941, he ignored orders for a defensive campaign and drove the startled British eastward to the Egyptian border in just two weeks. Although increasingly outnumbered, for many months he retained the upper hand with a combination of deception (once making dummy tanks on the back of Volkswagens), carefully marshaled defenses, and intrepid armored advances behind the front line.

Rommel won the respect and affection of many men who served under him. He demanded much, but never more than he was prepared to give himself. And he was lucky, too, something essential to all successful leaders. Once, during the desert war, he remained behind the Allied lines undetected in his staff car all night.

Rommel at Tobruk, North Africa, 1942. Speed of thought and action earned him the nickname "the Desert Fox."

Field Marshal Albert Kesselring (1885–1960)

Kesselring was probably the only German general whose reputation can stand comparison with Rommel's. In order to join the newly formed *Luftwaffe*, he learned to fly at the age of forty-eight and commanded air forces with great skill until 1941, when he was moved to the Mediterranean. After working beside Rommel in North Africa, he masterminded the brilliant German resistance in Italy against vastly larger and better-equipped forces. He arrived at the Western Front in March 1945, too late to affect the outcome of the war, and he surrendered to the Americans two months later.

Almost uniquely, Rommel won admiration from foe as well as friend. He was seen as a "decent" warrior, a gentleman who abided by the rules of war. British commanders felt so threatened by his brilliant reputation that they took deliberate steps to contradict it. Even Churchill has been accused of falling for the Rommel myth—it has been suggested that Singapore fell to the Japanese because the prime minister diverted a disproportionate amount of resources to North Africa to counter the threat to the Suez Canal posed by the dreaded "Desert Fox."

Meal on the move—Rommel has a quick bowl of soup during maneuvers through France in 1940. He won the respect of many of his soldiers by never asking them to endure any hardship he was not also prepared to endure himself.

Rommel (right) with his führer, 1942. Two years later, Rommel committed suicide after being associated with the failed plot to assassinate Hitler.

No leader, however successful, is without his critics, and Rommel is no exception. He was a fine battle tactician but because he never commanded at the highest level, his overall strategic and logistical skills were never tested. It is also said that, in the end, he was defeated in North Africa because he asked his forces to do more than they were capable of doing. (In his defense it should be pointed out that, overwhelmingly outnumbered and out-gunned, he had little choice.) Nor was he always an easy man to work with. His unpredictability and willingness to disobey orders caused serious problems for superiors trying to work to an overall strategic plan.

In July 1944, following the Allied landings in Normandy, Rommel wrote to Hitler suggesting that, as Germany was certain to lose the war, they should bring the fighting to an end as soon as possible. Knowing of the plot to kill the führer, Rommel was giving him a last chance to save his country, and himself.

The troops are fighting heroically everywhere, but the unequal struggle is nearing its end. I must beg you to draw the conclusions [i.e. sue for peace] without delay. I feel it is my duty as Commander-in-Chief of the Army Group to state this clearly.

Hans Speidel, *We Defended Normandy*

However, these are minor points—Rommel was an outstanding tactician, a respected commander, and a feared enemy. Ironically, ultimate recognition came for Rommel at the very end of his life. Fearing a popular backlash if the truth were known about Rommel's death, Hitler falsified accounts and granted a hero's farewell to a man who had turned against him.

Such was the esteem in which Rommel was held that the true nature of his death was suppressed and he was given a state funeral. Here, large crowds watch as his coffin, draped in the Nazi flag, is carried from the Ulm town hall.

The end of a national hero

On July 17, 1944, Rommel's staff car was attacked by a British fighter plane. He was taken to hospital with serious head injuries. Three days later the July Bomb Plot to assassinate Hitler failed. When Rommel, a close friend of many of the conspirators, came under suspicion, Hitler gave him the choice of facing charges or taking poison. He chose the latter and died on October 14. Because he was such a popular figure, the German government announced that he had died of wounds and granted him the honor of a state funeral.

President Franklin D. Roosevelt (1882–1945)

Roosevelt was the only elected head of a major state to survive the transition from peacetime to war. With notable political skill, he guided the United States out of isolationism and into its new role as a military superpower committed to leading the Allies to victory. In addition, more than any other leader, he gave the war a moral dimension. Although obliged to fight as an ally of the communist USSR, he always insisted that the United States was not involved in a mere power struggle but in a crusade for freedom. The sudden outbreak of war, following the surprise Japanese attack on Pearl Harbor in December 1941, was not Roosevelt's first great test. He had been elected president in 1932 to solve the country's biggest ever peacetime crisis—the Great Depression. He acted swiftly and passed on his quiet confidence to the nation, most memorably in "fireside chats" on the radio.

He did not have the firecracker leadership style of Hitler; nor did he have Churchill's skills as a speech-maker, but he was no less effective. The majority of Americans developed sufficient faith in Roosevelt's abilities to re-elect him in 1936, 1940, and 1944, and they went to war under a tried and trusted leader.

Right: Franklin D. Roosevelt, the only U.S. president to be re-elected three times

Roosevelt during his successful 1932 presidential election campaign. Because he was partially disabled after an attack of polio, he was rarely photographed below the waist.

Roosevelt, a fine speaker on the radio, was never more eloquent than when he addressed the American people shortly after his country had joined the war:

We will not, under any threat, or in the face of any danger, surrender the guarantees of liberty our forefathers framed for us in our Bill of Rights ... We are solemnly determined that no power or combination of powers on this earth shall shake our hold upon them. We covenant with each other before all the world, that having taken up arms in the defense of liberty, we will not lay them down before liberty is once again secure in the world we live in. For that security we pray; for that security we act now and evermore.

Broadcast to the nation on the 150th anniversary of the adoption of the American Bill of Rights, December 15, 1941

Roosevelt despised Nazism and all it stood for. Had he been a free agent, he would probably have joined the struggle against Hitler in 1940. But, like all great leaders, he knew he had to take his followers with him. And, until Pearl Harbor, the majority of Americans were uncommitted to what they believed was a European conflict. In the meantime, Roosevelt did what he could to assist Hitler's enemies. He showed public support for Churchill, with whom he drew up an optimistic blueprint for the postwar world (the Atlantic Charter); he persuaded Congress to pass the Lend-Lease Act; and he permitted American warships to be swapped for British naval bases.

The U.S. naval base at Pearl Harbor, Hawaii, after the sudden Japanese air attack that finally persuaded Americans to join the war

Lend-Lease

In the 1940 presidential election, Roosevelt campaigned successfully on a pledge to keep the United States out of the war. He can hardly have believed this was possible. Indeed, shortly afterward, he asked Congress to pass a Lend-Lease Bill giving him power to subsidize the war effort of countries upon which the United States depended for her security. This blatant support for Great Britain and her allies, which Congress debated for months before accepting, was as close as Roosevelt could come to entering the conflict without actually committing fighting forces.

General George Patton (1885–1945)

Tough, controversial, and flamboyant, Patton was perhaps America's most charismatic land commander. Converted to high-speed tank warfare during World War I, he put his skills to devastating effect in North Africa, Sicily, and, most noticeably, Northern Europe. His rapid advances across France to Lorraine (1944) and then to the borders of Czechoslovakia (1945) were among the Allies' most spectacular offensives. Although adored by his men, Patton could be awkward and insensitive. He maintained a fruitless rivalry with Montgomery and, in 1943, was temporarily demoted for slapping an exhausted young soldier.

Admiral Ernest King (1878–1956)

The abrasive Admiral King, more than any other leader, was responsible for the Allied victory in the Pacific. Having experience in carrier command, he was ideally placed to increase and reorganize the U.S. fleet after Pearl Harbor and to re-train it in the tactics of air and amphibious warfare. His fierce advocacy of the Pacific war and determination to have his own way frequently brought him into conflict with politicians, generals, and fellow admirals. Nevertheless, by 1945 he had turned the U.S. Navy into the huge yet efficient modern fighting force that brought victory over Japan and left the United States undisputed ruler of the world's oceans.

A U.S. propaganda poster calling for an increase in arms production. The swastika target was controversial—many Americans believed they should be concentrating their resources against Japan.

When war came, Roosevelt faced four main tasks. First, he had to see that massive American resources were mobilized swiftly and efficiently. Using government agencies, he had begun preparing for war in 1939. By 1942, U.S. war production equaled that of Japan and Germany; two years later it was double.

Second, Roosevelt had to ensure he was served by the best advisers and commanders, while taking ultimate responsibility for their actions. He was a sound judge of character, as shown by the faith he put in Eisenhower. As well as handling more fiery commanders (like Admiral King) with considerable skill, he was prepared to make and stick by difficult strategic decisions, such as giving the European theater priority over the Pacific, and agreeing to the development of the atomic bomb.

43

Roosevelt found his third task, building and maintaining an alliance of allies, the most taxing. He had some personal liking for Churchill (much exaggerated by Churchill himself) but was uncomfortable fighting a war to maintain the British empire. He was equally unhappy fighting alongside the tyrant Stalin. Although diplomacy and U.S. aid held the Allies together for the duration of the war, Roosevelt seems to have misjudged the Soviet dictator. When plans for democratic governments in postwar Eastern Europe were agreed at the Yalta Conference (February 1945), Roosevelt unwisely believed Stalin's idea of democracy was similar to his own.

In his last task of providing firm leadership without overstepping the bounds of democracy, Roosevelt excelled. His critics claimed his manner verged on the dictatorial, but the majority of Americans stuck by him and, in November 1944, re-elected him president for a fourth term. This unprecedented mark of approval, received only a few months before his death, was a fitting tribute to the war leader who helped to ensure the survival of liberty in the postwar world.

General Douglas MacArthur (1880–1964)

Having retired from the army in 1937, MacArthur was recalled to active duty in July 1941. He showed considerable intelligence, skill, and resolution in commanding U.S. forces in the subsequent Southwest Pacific campaign against Japan. Appointed commander of all US Army forces in the Pacific in 1945, he organized the Japanese surrender on September 2 and, as commander of the Allied occupation of Japan from 1945 to 1951, played a major part in demobilizing the country and establishing a modern democracy.

President Franklin D. Roosevelt

Lieutenant-General Carl Spaatz,
Commander of the U.S. Strategic Air
Forces in Europe

General Carl Spaatz
(1891–1974)

Many of the Allied land campaigns owed
their success to the deft command of air
power provided by Spaatz. He observed the
Battle of Great Britain at first hand and
returned to Europe to direct the American
arm of the Allied bombing offensive. After
commanding U.S. air forces in the North
African, Sicilian, and Italian campaigns, he
helped plan the air force's role in the
Normandy landings of 1944. He ended his
wartime career in charge of the bombing
offensive against Japan that culminated in
the atomic bomb attacks on Hiroshima and
Nagasaki.

Left: Roosevelt and Churchill on board
the battleship Prince of Wales, *in*
1941. Churchill made much of
his close relationship with the U.S.
president, although Roosevelt was
less enthusiastic.

Joseph Stalin (1879–1953)

Stalin was arguably World War II's most successful head of state. Together, he and Hitler were the most unpleasant and ruthless leaders. He endured the German onslaught of Operation Barbarossa and went on to rally his people and lead them to eventual victory in what the Russians called the Great Patriotic War. By the summer of 1945, the successes of the Red Army and Stalin's tough, scheming diplomacy had raised the status of the USSR from pariah among nations to a superpower matched only by the United States.

Right: Joseph Stalin (Stalin means "Man of Steel"), arguably the greatest tyrant of the twentieth century

Stalin's war got off to the worst possible start when his armies were smashed by the German invaders. In late 1941, with German troops only a few miles from Moscow, a train was ready to take Stalin to the east and possibly to his downfall. The dire situation was partly of his own making. His paranoid purge of suspected opponents in 1938 had removed 10,000 senior army commanders. The void had not been even half filled by 1941, when the Red Army was desperately short of experienced field commanders.

As Stalin had reacted to the German attack by appointing himself prime minister and supreme army commander, he must also take responsibility for the failings of the USSR's high command at

Anger, not surprise

Stalin was not totally surprised by the Nazi attack of June 1941. Many intelligence services had warned that it was about to take place and he had never believed the Nazi–Soviet Pact of August 1939 would last. Nevertheless, he was furious. He was humiliated by Hitler's sweeping victories and irritated he hadn't had more time to organize resistance. During the previous months, he had done everything in his power to delay the invasion—even showing his friendship for Hitler by providing him with war supplies!

Russian troops defending Leningrad, 1942. Stalin's pre-war purge of thousands of experienced officers left his army at a serious disadvantage when the Germans invaded in 1941.

this crucial juncture. Some say that he panicked, and there were rumors that he had fled into exile. He did not make his authority properly felt until he teamed up with Zhukov to save Moscow and drive the Germans back.

That said, Stalin was not entirely to blame for his catastrophic position in the summer of 1941. During the 1930s, he had repeatedly warned Great Britain and France of the Nazi threat. To his obvious irritation, their response was lukewarm and they rejected his offer of an anti-German alliance. Stalin certainly did not want war. Western caution forced him into the Nazi–Soviet Pact of August 1939. This freed Hitler to face the Western Allies with confidence, but, when they were almost defeated, he turned on the USSR.

The paranoid leader—a German cartoon mocks Stalin's fear of internal opposition by showing him fighting himself with hammer and sickle.

Broadcasting in July 1941, Stalin typically stirred up hatred for Germany while justifying the Nazi–Soviet Pact of August 1939:

How could the Soviet Government have consented to ... a Non-Aggression Pact with such treacherous fiends as Hitler and Ribbentrop? Was this not an error ... of the Soviet Government? Of course not! ... I think that not a single peace-loving state could decline a peace treaty with a neighboring state, even though the latter was headed by such fiends and cannibals as Hitler and Ribbentrop ... What did we gain by concluding the Non-Aggression Pact ... ? We secured ... peace for a year and a half, and the opportunity of preparing ... to repulse fascist Germany should she risk an attack on our country...

Broadcast to the people of the Soviet Union, July 3, 1941

German troops surrendering during a Soviet counterattack outside Moscow, April 1942

From 1942 onward, Stalin matured as a war leader. He recognized able battle commanders and, unlike Hitler, learned not to interfere in what they were doing. This left officers like Zhukov and Konev with a relatively free hand to manage their campaigns as they saw fit. Stalin's determination never to surrender also played a part in turning the war on the Eastern Front. His methods were ruthless in the extreme (for example, ordering his soldiers to take "not a step back" and establishing units behind the front line to shoot them if they did) but they worked.

Marshal Ivan Konev (1897–1973)

Stalin was fortunate that a man of Konev's abilities survived the purges to lead resistance to the German invasion of 1941. After playing a key role in the defense of Moscow, he was even more impressive leading counteroffensives in 1943–45. Commanding a force that eventually totaled one million men, he drove through Poland and across Germany to Berlin itself. Much decorated for his outstanding leadership, after the war he replaced Zhukov as supreme commander of the USSR's forces on land.

49

Kulaks (rich peasants) being deported from their farms on Stalin's orders in 1930. Policies such as these, as well as showing inhuman cruelty, seriously set back the USSR's economic development.

Stalin's ruthlessness, like Hitler's, could also be detrimental to the war effort. While generally successful at uniting Russians behind him, his pointless cruelty toward the USSR's minority peoples frequently deprived him of potential support. He wasted valuable resources, for example, deporting countless families from the Ukraine and Kazakhstan merely because they had accepted German occupation.

Vyacheslav Molotov (1890–1986)

As the USSR's foreign minister (1939–52), Molotov's influence on Soviet diplomacy during the war was second only to Stalin's. He helped formulate the Nazi–Soviet Peace Pact of 1939 and was working on a closer alliance with the Axis when Operation Barbarossa forced a total re-think of his policies. Undaunted, he swiftly came to agreements with Churchill and Roosevelt. Advising Stalin in the Allied conferences at Tehran (1943), Yalta, and Potsdam (both 1945), he helped determine the nature of the postwar world.

It was perhaps as a diplomat that Stalin most surprised. Although he failed to persuade the Allies to open a "Second Front" in Northwest Europe until 1944, he got his way in most other areas using an explosive mix of flattery, argument, deceit, and bullying. At one stage he even hinted that he might strike a new accord with Hitler. He drove a wedge between Churchill and Roosevelt, and almost convinced the American president that the Soviet leader was a man of his word. As a result, the war left him not only master of the USSR but also potentially of a vast area of Eastern Europe that he was to forge into the communist Eastern Bloc.

Unspeakable atrocities were committed by both sides during the Russo-German war of 1941–45. While denying any wrongdoing on the part of the Red Army, Stalin came close to encouraging barbarity:

Sometimes the foreign press engages in prattle ... that the Soviet people hate the Germans just because they are Germans ... and that therefore the Red Army does not take German soldiers prisoner. This is, of course, a ... stupid lie. ... Certainly the Red Army must annihilate the German fascist occupants, since they wish to enslave our motherland, and when, being surrounded by our troops, they refuse to ... surrender, the Red Army annihilates them ... War is war.

Stalin's "Order of the Day" on the 24th anniversary of the Red Army, released by the Soviet embassy in Washington, D.C., as an Information Bulletin, February 23, 1942.

The Red Army enters Berlin, April 1945. Determined that Germany should not recover her former might, Stalin ensured that the country (and its capital) was partitioned among the Allies.

What are we to make of such a leader? On a personal level he was a heartless, paranoid monster, a bully, liar, cheat, coward, and tyrant. Yet, revolting though his methods might have been, he achieved victory. Somehow, at horrific cost, he put the dark winter of 1941–42 behind him, broke the German spirit at Stalingrad, and saw his troops beat the British and Americans to Berlin. In purely military terms, it was the most remarkable achievement of any war leader.

General Hideki Tojo (1884–1948)

Alone among the major warring nations, Japan produced no supreme wartime leader who caught the public imagination. This was largely due to the tradition of absolute loyalty to the head of state, the Emperor. No subject was prepared to put himself in a position that might challenge Hirohito's supreme and divine position. Within that constraint, General Tojo, the Japanese prime minister from October 1941 to July 1944, came closer than anyone else to exercising individual control over Japan's war effort.

General Hideki Tojo, Japan's unspectacular but efficient wartime prime minister

Tojo was not a flamboyant leader. Essentially a bureaucrat and politician, he wielded power as a schemer and organizer. What distinguished him from most of his colleagues was his fanatical nationalism. He concentrated huge power into his own hands in an effort to turn the dream of a Japanese-led, self-sufficient "East Asia Co-Prosperity Sphere" into reality.

The idea of the Co-Prosperity Sphere was part of the "New Order For East Asia" announced by Prime Minister Prince Konoe in 1938. It was heralded as an anti-communist, anti-imperialist pact between Japan, China, and Manchuko (the Japanese puppet state of Manchuria in northern China). But to non-Japanese, the Sphere seemed merely a smoke-screen for the creation of a Japanese Asian Empire. These fears were given further substance when Japan's later conquests were incorporated into a "Greater East Asia Co-Prosperity Sphere."

Having served as deputy chief of staff in the Kwantung Army occupying Manchuko, in 1938 Tojo returned to Japan as deputy war minister. By 1940, now the principal war minister, he headed the cabinet "Control Faction" calling for a "New Structure Movement." This sought a one-party state and a controlled economy in order to maximize the country's potential. The links with European fascist thinking were reinforced when Japan, supported by Tojo, made a pact with Germany and Italy in 1940.

Tojo's passionate faith in Japan's imperial destiny gave his policies a powerful, if superficial, appeal. In October 1941, he replaced the more cautious Konoe as prime minister. Emperor Hirohito, fearing that Tojo was allowing his nationalist zeal to cloud his judgment, advised him to seek an accord with the United States. But to Tojo, war with the United States was an inevitable part of his plan, and he backed the fateful attack on Pearl Harbor in December 1941.

President Chiang Kai-Shek (1887–1975)

The first fighting in what would become part of World War II took place when the Japanese invaded eastern China in 1937. China's Nationalist president, General Chiang Kai-shek, was swiftly defeated and withdrew inland. Although allied to the United States from December 1941 onward, he failed to make much headway against the invader. After Japan's surrender, Chiang split with the communists, who defeated his forces and drove him from the mainland to Formosa (Taiwan) in 1949.

Pearl Harbor, December 7, 1941. U.S. servicemen watch in disbelief as the great American naval base is bombarded by Japanese aircraft.

Tojo was now at the height of his powers. He was prime minister, war minister, and, from 1943, minister of commerce and industry. He manipulated elections and dominated the cabinet. In February 1944, to get a closer control over strategic planning, he made himself chief-of-staff. As long as Japanese forces remained victorious, his power seemed unassailable.

As Tojo suggested in his speech to graduates from the Manchuko Imperial University, nothing inspired the Japanese more than loyalty to the emperor and the imperial ethos:

Never before has your service been more urgently needed. I earnestly hope that, whatever difficulties you encounter, you will not spare yourselves in your determination to kindle within you the spirit of Imperial Japan. Heralded by our wonderful victories in the Greater East Asia War, see how the Imperial Spirit is flourishing! Never lose sight of it, for only when you have taken it to your hearts will you be able to play your full part.

Speech broadcast on September 25, 1942, and picked up by the U.S. Foreign Broadcast Monitoring Service

Honor in death—Japanese suicide pilots (kamikaze) *attack a U.S. carrier in April 1945.*

The tide turned decisively in mid-1944. Tojo had failed to win support from Japan's new colonies. He had not given sufficient attention to updating army material—tanks that had easily crushed the Chinese in the 1930s, for example, were hopelessly inadequate against the Americans. And he had insisted, again against Hirohito's advice, in pursuing the war against the United States when the possibility of victory was receding with each passing month.

On July 16, 1944, following the U.S. invasion of Saipan, Tojo was replaced as chief of staff. Four days later, he and all his cabinet resigned. Like Hitler and Mussolini, Tojo had discovered too late that successful leadership involves tempering bright dreams with sober practicality.

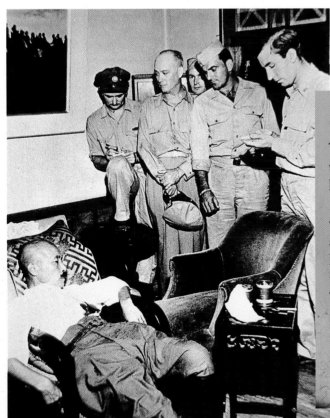

At the scene of Tojo's suicide attempt in 1945

Ignominious end

To avoid being arrested by the Americans, Tojo shot himself on September 11, 1945. Although badly wounded, he did not die and was nursed back to health. Seven months later, the International Military Tribunal for the Far East put him on trial as a war criminal. He was found guilty and was hanged on December 23, 1948.

Marshal George Zhukov (1896–1974)

By the end of the war, Zhukov had established a reputation as one of the most able Allied commanders. Certainly he had achieved much, playing a major role in almost every Soviet campaign of the war, from the defense of Moscow in 1941 to the capture of Berlin in 1945. Some actions, particularly early on, he handled with marked skill. But like his commander, Stalin, he was also adept at taking sole credit for victories that owed as much to others' efforts. Furthermore, his strategy often relied on battering the enemy into submission with overwhelming force rather than outwitting them.

Zhukov was a professional soldier through and through. Recruited into the Czar's army in World War I, he had joined the Red Army in 1918 and fought in the Russian Civil War. Between the wars, he trained in both Russia and Germany before ably commanding Soviet forces against Japan in 1939. From here, he moved to the Finnish front, then back to Kiev, before being made the Red Army's chief of staff in January 1941.

The German invasion of 1941 brought the best out of Zhukov. His arrival in Leningrad in September raised morale and led to an improvement in the city's defenses. A month later he was back in Moscow, where he was made commander-in-chief of the Western Front and told to defend the city at all costs. Although he made the best of the resources at his disposal, his strongest ally was probably the weather ("General Winter"), for which the Germans were woefully ill-prepared. Zhukov's masterstroke was an unexpected counteroffensive in early December. Exhausted, outnumbered, and often literally freezing to death, the Germans fell back from the capital.

Toasting their triumph— Marshal Zhukov (center) raises his glass with Montgomery, Eisenhower, and other Allied leaders at a gathering in New York City to celebrate victory in Europe in 1945.

Right: Boris Ugarov's garish representation of the defense of Stalingrad, 1942

Field Marshal Friedrich Von Paulus (1890–1957)

Von Paulus, one of the principal planners of Operation Barbarossa, led the German 6th Army in the attack on Stalingrad in August 1942. Having fought his way into the ruined city at enormous cost, he was cut off by Zhukov's counterattack. Hitler forbade him to surrender. Eventually, with two-thirds of his men lost and no hope of rescue, he disobeyed orders and surrendered. Publicly condemned by Hitler, Paulus later made anti-Nazi broadcasts and testified against German war criminals in the Nuremberg War Trials.

Stalin worked closely with Zhukov and developed a grudging respect for the marshal's abilities. Zhukov was said to be the only man who could contradict the paranoid dictator and remain alive. The two men shared certain characteristics. Both learned to pass responsibility to officers at the front and both had a cold disregard for individual lives. As Stalin was prepared to sacrifice thousands to achieve a political aim, so would Zhukov in his ruthless pursuit of victory.

During the war, each combatant nation threw up its own style of leader. Just as a decent diplomat like Eisenhower would probably have made little headway in the USSR, so Zhukov's single-minded ruthlessness would not have been acceptable in the U.S. Army. But on the Eastern Front, awash with cruelty and suffering, his methods served their purpose and even won his soldiers' grudging admiration. By 1944, when German resources were stretched to breaking point, he advanced right along the entire front in the sure knowledge that, whatever his losses, the Germans could not possibly resist for long.

The Battle of Kursk, 1943

Zhukov masterminded the crushing Soviet victory at the Battle of Kursk, often claimed as the largest tank battle in history (perhaps over 5,000 tanks took part). Learning of a proposed German attack on a bulge in the Soviet line around the town of Kursk, Zhukov built up the area's defenses to absorb the German assault and planned a massive counterattack. The strategy, executed in the field by Generals Popov and Sokolovsky, worked well and, by the end of July, the Soviet armies were advancing along a broad front.

Soviet tanks on their way to the Kursk salient where they took part in the greatest tank battle of all time

When victory was assured, Zhukov, who always had a keen eye for glory, returned to the front to take personal command of the offensive in the Ukraine. Massive armored thrusts, supported by artillery and rocket attack, drove the enemy back into Hungary, then into Poland, Czechoslovakia (now the Czech Republic and the Slovak Republic), and finally into Germany itself. In April 1945, he personally supervised the assault on Berlin and represented the USSR at Germany's official surrender on May 8.

Zhukov's finest hour—in a reconstructed photograph, Soviet troops hoist the red flag over Berlin. Later, fearful of his marshal's popular success, Stalin had Zhukov removed from the limelight.

The Price of Victory

In 1945, Zhukov returned to Moscow a popular hero. Leading the victory parade in Moscow's Red Square on a white charger, it seemed as if he could do no wrong. But he had already done wrong—he had aroused the jealousy of Stalin. The Soviet dictator wished to be heralded as the sole architect of victory. Accordingly, Zhukov was moved out of the limelight and held only minor military commands until Stalin's death in 1953, when the new regime appointed him minister of defense.

Date list

1937
July 7 — Japanese invasion of China.

1938
July 28 — Soviet and Japanese troops clash in Manchuria.

Nov 3 — Japan announces New Order for Southeast Asia.

1939
March 15 — Hitler invades Czechoslovakia.

May 22 — Hitler signs "Pact of Steel" with Mussolini.

Aug 23 — Nazi–Soviet Non-Aggression Pact.

Sept 1 — Hitler invades Poland.

Sept 3 — Great Britain , France, and their empires declare war on Germany.

Sept 5 — Roosevelt proclaims U.S. neutrality.

Nov 8 — Failed attempt to assassinate Hitler.

Nov 30 — Stalin invades Finland (peace made March 12, 1940).

1940
April 9 — Hitler invades Denmark and Norway.

May 10 — Hitler invades France, Belgium, Luxemburg, and the Netherlands. Churchill becomes Prime Minister of Great Britain.

June 10 — Mussolini declares war on Great Britain and France.

June 22 — Pètain, the French Prime Minister, signs armistice with Hitler.

June 28 — Great Britain recognizes de Gaulle as leader of Free French.

July 10 — Battle of Britain begins.

Aug 3 — Italy invades British Somaliland in East Africa.

Sept 13 — Mussolini invades Egypt.

Sept 16 — United States Military Conscription Bill passed.

Sept 27 — Axis Pact signed by Germany, Italy, and Japan.

Oct 28 — Mussolini invades Greece.

Nov 5 — Roosevelt re-elected as U.S. president.

Nov 22 — Greeks defeat Italian 9th Army.

1941
Jan 22 — British take Tobruk, North Africa.

Feb 12 — Rommel arrives in Tripoli, North Africa.

March 11 — President Roosevelt signs the Lend-Lease Act.

April 6 — Hitler invades Greece and Yugoslavia.

April 14 — Rommel attacks Tobruk.

April 17 — Yugoslavia surrenders to Germany.

April 27 — Greece surrenders to Germany.

June 22 — Operation Barbarossa begins.

July 26 — Roosevelt suspends U.S. relations with Japan.

Aug 12 — Roosevelt and Churchill sign Atlantic Charter.

Aug 20 — Siege of Leningrad begins.

Oct 2 (to Dec 5) — German attack on Moscow.

Oct 17 — Tojo becomes Prime Minister of Japan.

Dec 7 — Japanese attack U.S. base at Pearl Harbor, Hawaii.

Dec 8 — U.S. and Great Britain declare war on Japan.

Dec 11 — Hitler declares war on U.S.

Dec 19 — Hitler takes command of German Army.

1942
Feb 15 — Singapore falls to the Japanese.

May 4–8 — Battle of Coral Sea begins

June 4 — Battle of Midway begins (to June 6).

June 9 — Japanese conquest of the Philippines complete.

June 21 — Rommel captures Tobruk.

June 25 — Eisenhower arrives in London.

July 1-30 — First Battle of El Alamein.

Aug 7	Montgomery takes command of British Army in North Africa.	**July 20**	Assassination attempt on Hitler fails. Tojo resigns as Japanese prime minister.
Aug 12	Stalin and Churchill meet in Moscow.	**Aug 25**	Liberation of Paris.
Sept 13 (to Feb 2, 1943)	Battle of Stalingrad.	**Oct 14**	Rommel commits suicide.
Nov 1	Montgomery breaks through at El Alamein.	**Oct 20**	U.S. troops land in the Philippines.
Nov 8	Operation Torch: Allied invasion of North Africa.	**Nov 24**	French capture Strasbourg.
		Dec 16-27	Battle of the Bulge in the Ardennes.
1943			
Jan 10	Zhukov's counteroffensive at Stalingrad.	**1945**	
		Jan 17	Soviets enter Warsaw.
Jan 24	Roosevelt and Churchill meet at Casablanca Conference.	**Feb 4-11**	Roosevelt, Churchill, and Stalin meet at Yalta Conference.
May 13	German and Italian troops surrender in North Africa.	**Feb 13/14**	Allied bombing raid destroys Dresden in a firestorm.
July 5	German offensive at Kursk repulsed by Zhukov.	**Feb 25**	Massive U.S. firebomb attack on Tokyo.
July 9/10	Allied landing in Sicily.	**March 7**	Allies cross the Rhine.
July 25	Mussolini arrested.	**April 1**	U.S. troops land on Okinawa.
July 27/28	Allied air raid causes firestorm in Hamburg.	**April 12**	President Roosevelt dies. Truman becomes U.S. President.
Sept 11	Germans occupy Rome.		
Sept 12	Germans rescue Mussolini.	**April 16**	Zhukov attacks Berlin.
Nov 6	Russians recapture Kiev in the Ukraine.	**April 28**	Mussolini hanged by Italian partisans.
Nov 28	Roosevelt, Churchill, and Stalin meet at Tehran Conference.	**April 30**	Hitler commits suicide.
		May 8	VE (Victory in Europe) Day.
1944		**May 23**	Himmler commits suicide.
Jan 6	Soviet troops reach Poland.	**July 16**	Potsdam Conference begins.
June 5	Allies enter Rome.	**July 26**	Attlee succeeds Churchill as British Prime Minister.
June 6	D-Day landings.		
June 17	U.S. troops land on Saipan, Marianas. U.S. Air Force bombs mainland Japan.	**Aug 6**	Atomic bomb dropped on Hiroshima, Japan.
		Aug 8	Stalin declares war on Japan.
June 27	U.S. troops capture Cherbourg.	**Aug 9**	Atomic bomb dropped on Nagasaki, Japan.
July 9	British and Canadian troops capture Caen.	**Aug 15**	VJ (Victory over Japan) Day.
		Nov 20	Nuremberg war crimes trials begin.

Glossary

Abyssinia Former name of Ethiopia.

Allies Members of the anti-Axis alliance, led by Great Britain and the United States.

Appeasement Prewar Franco-British policy of non-confrontation with Hitler.

Atlantic Charter Declaration of aims for the postwar world, drawn up by Roosevelt and Churchill in August 1941.

Autocrat Leader not restrained by a political party, cabinet or parliament.

Axis Wartime alliance of Germany, Italy, and Japan.

Battle of the Bulge Largest U.S. land battle of the war and last major German offensive, fought in the Ardennes in December 1944.

Cabinet Organ of central government headed by a prime minister.

Coalition government Government made up of members of different political parties.

Convoy Many ships sailing together for greater security.

Diplomacy Art of negotiation, usually between states.

Eastern Bloc Area of Eastern Europe dominated by the USSR after the war.

Fascist Loose term, originally used in Italy but later in Germany, for a non-democratic form of government based on fervent nationalism and strong central control under an all-powerful leader.

Free French Forces Forces commanded by de Gaulle that continued the war against the Axis after the French government had made peace in June 1940.

Führer German leader, i.e., Hitler

General Staff Military officers advising senior commanders on strategy.

Gestapo Nazi secret police.

Isolationism A policy of not taking part in the affairs of other countries.

Luftwaffe German Air Force.

Martial law Law imposed by military force rather than the courts.

Material Army's equipment and munitions.

Nazi German National Socialist Party.

Nazi–Soviet Pact Agreement between Germany and the USSR, made in August 1939, not to go to war with each other.

Operation Barbarossa Code name for German invasion of the USSR in June 1941.

Operation Overlord Code name for Allied invasion of Northwest Europe in June 1944.

Operation Torch Code name for Anglo-American invasion of Northwest Africa in November 1942.

Panzers German armored or tank forces capable of high-speed offensives.

Pearl Harbor U.S. naval base in Hawaii attacked by Japan without warning in December 1941.

Phony war Lull in the fighting in Northwest Europe following the invasion of Poland in September 1939. It was ended by the German offensives of April–May 1940.

Potsdam Conference Last major Allied conference of the war, attended by Stalin, U.S. President Truman, and (for a time) Churchill, to discuss the reconstruction of war-torn Europe.

Second Front Allied offensive against Germany in Northwest Europe, eventually launched in June 1944.

Soviet Belonging to the USSR.

SS (*Schutzstaffel*) Originally Hitler's private guard, it was developed by Himmler into a private army and huge business enterprise.

Strategy Art of campaigning, or planning a campaign, with any branch of the armed forces.

Tactics Maneuvers in the face of an enemy.

Tehran Conference Meeting of Stalin, Roosevelt, and Churchill in December 1943 to discuss war aims and strategy.

Third Reich Hitler's Nazi empire.

USSR Union of Soviet Socialist Republics, the Russian-dominated state that replaced the Russian Empire and lasted until 1990.

Yalta Conference Second meeting of the "Big Three" (Stalin, Roosevelt, and Churchill), held in February 1945 to discuss strategy and the nature of the postwar world.

Resources

Books to read

Kitchen, M. *A World in Flames: A Short History of the Second World War in Europe*. Addison-Wesley Publishing, Co., 1990.

Stalcup, Brenda, ed. *Adolf Hitler* (People Who Made History). Greenhaven Press, 2000.

Joseph, Paul. *Dwight D. Eisenhower* (U.S. Presidents). Checkerboard Library, 1999.

Freedman, Russell. *Franklin Delano Roosevelt*. Clarion Books, 1992.

Sources

Stephen E. Ambrose, *Eisenhower: Soldier and President*. Touchstone, 1991.

Courtney Browne, *Tojo: The Last Banzai*. Da Capo, 1998.

Alan Bullock, *Hitler, A Study in Tyranny*. HarperCollins, 1994.

Alan Bullock, *Hitler and Stalin: Parallel Lives*. Vintage Books, 1993.

P. Calvocoressi, G. Wint & J. Pritchard, *Total War: the Causes and Course of the Second World War*. Viking, 1989.

Winston Churchill, *The Second World War*, (6 vols). Houghton Mifflin, 1986.

Martin Gilbert, *The Second World War*. Henry Holt, 1992.

B. H. Liddell Hart, *History of the Second World War*. Cassell, 1970.

David Irving, *The Trail of the Fox: The Life of Field-Marshal Rommel*. Wordsworth, 1999.

Edvard Radzinsky, *Stalin*. Anchor, 1997.

D. Mack Smith, *Mussolini*. Random House, 1983.

William J. Spahr, *Zhukov: The Rise and Fall of a Great Captain*. Presidio, 1995.

E-A. Wheal, S. Pope & J. Taylor, *A Dictionary of the Second World War*. Grafton, 1989.

Charles Williams, *The Last Great Frenchman: A Life of General De Gaulle*. John Wiley, 1997.

Websites

There are dozens of websites with information on World War II leaders. These might be suitable starting places.

Primary sources:
The Mount Holyoke College website—an excellent selection of World War II documents:
www.mtholyoke.edu/acad/intrel/ww2.htm

Internet Modern History Sourcebook:
www.fordham.edu/halsall/mod/modsbook.html

The Avalon Project at the Yale Law School, Documents in Law, History and Diplomacy:
www.yale.edu/lawweb/avalon/avalon.htm

Other:
Canadian Forces College - good on the military:
www.cfcsc.dnd.ca/links/milhist/wwii.html
The BBC has all kinds of interesting material:
www.bbc.co.uk/education/history

Index

If a number is in **bold** type, there is an illustration

Alexander, Field Marshal Harold 14, 24, 25, 26
Aosta, Duke of 30
Auchinleck, General Claude 24, 25

Berlin 51, **51**, 59, **59**
Bradley, General Omar 16, 26, 27
Bulge, Battle of the 17, 26

Chamberlain, Neville 7
Chiang Kai-Shek, General 53
China 53
Churchill, Winston 4, 5, 6, **6**, 7, **7**, 8, **8**, 9, **9**, 10, **10**, 11, **11**, 13, 14, 34, 37, 51
    Roosevelt and 8, **9**, 10, 11, 42, **44**, 50

D-Day landings 15, **15**, 16, **16**
Dachau concentration camp **22**
Darlan, Admiral Jean 14
De Gaulle, Charles 14, 17

East Africa 31
Eisenhower, Dwight D. 12, **12**, 13, **13**, 14, **14**, 15, **15**, 16, **16**, 17, 26, **26**, 27, 43, **56**
El Alamein 24, 25, **25**

fascism 28, 29, 30, 32, 33, 53
France 14, 15, 17, 48
Free French Forces 17

George VI, King 4
Germany 18, 20, 22, 23, 30, 33, 38, 53
    capture of Berlin 51, **51**, 59, **59**
    Peace Pact with USSR 48, 50
"Ghost Division" 34
Grand Alliance 8
Great Britain 6, 7, 8, 9, 10, 11, 24, 25, 26, 27, 48

Harris, Sir Arthur (Bomber) 7
Himmler, Heinrich 23, **23**

Hirohito, Emperor 4, 52, 53, 55
Hitler, Adolf **4**, 5, **5**, 8, 18, 19, **19**, 20, **20**, 21, 22, 23, **23**, 47
    and Mussolini 30, 31, **31**, 33
    and Paulus 57
    and Rommel 34, 38, **38**, 39

Italy 26, 28, 29, 30, 31, 32, 38, 53

Japan 40, 43, 44, 45, 52, 53, 54, 55
July Bomb Plot 22, 39

Kesselring, Field Marshal Albert 37
King, Admiral Ernest 43
Konev, Marshal Ivan 49
Konoe, Prince 52
kulaks **50**
Kursk, Battle of 58, **58**

MacArthur, General Douglas 13, 44
Marshall, George C. 13, 14
Molotov, Vyacheslav 50
Montgomery, Field Marshal Bernard 15, **15**, 16, 24, **24**, 25, **25**, 26, **26**, 27, **27**, 43, **56**
Mussolini, Benito 4, 28, **28**, 29, 30, **30**, 31, **31**, **32**, **33**, **35**

Nazi–Soviet Pact 46, 48, 50, 51
North Africa 13, 14, 24, 25, 35, 36, 37, 38

Operation Barbarossa 21, 57
Operation Overlord **14**, 15, 16, 17
Operation Torch 13, **13**, 14, **14**

Patton, General George 15, 16, **16**, 26, 27, 43
Paulus, Field Marshal Friedrich Von 57
Pearl Harbor 40, 42, **42**, 53, **53**

Rommel, Field Marshal Erwin 24, 25, 34, **34**, 35, **35**, 36, **36**, 37, **37**, 38, **38**, 39, **39**

Roosevelt, Franklin D. 4, 5, **5**, 13, 14, 40, **40**, 41, **41**, 42, 43, 44, **44**, 45
    Churchill and 8, 9, **9**, 10, 11, 42, 44, **44**, 50
Rundstedt, Field Marshal Karl Rudolf Gerd von 21
Russia, *see* USSR

"saturation bombing" 7
Second Front 50
7th Panzer Division 34
Sicily 15, 25, 26, 32
Spaatz, General Carl 45, **45**
Stalin, Joseph 4, 46, 47, **47**, 48, **48**, 49, 50, 51, **51**, 58, 59
    Churchill, Roosevelt and 9, 10, 11, **44**, 50
Stalingrad 51, 57, **57**
Stauffenberg, Count von 22
suicide pilots **54**, 55

Tehran Conference 9, 10, 50
Tojo, General Hideki 52, **52**, 53, 54, 55, **55**

United States 8, 12, 13, 14, 15, 16, 17, 40, 41, 42, 43, 44, 45, 53, 55
USSR 8, 46, 47, 48, 49, 50, 51, 56, 57, 58, 59
    capture of Berlin 51, **51**, 59, **59**
    German invasion 5, 20, 21, 46, 56, 57
    Peace Pact with Germany 46, 48, 50, 51

Victor Emanuel III, King 32, **32**, 33

Yalta Conference 9, **44**, 50

Zhukov, Marshal George 4, 8 46, 49, 56, **56**, 57, 58, 59